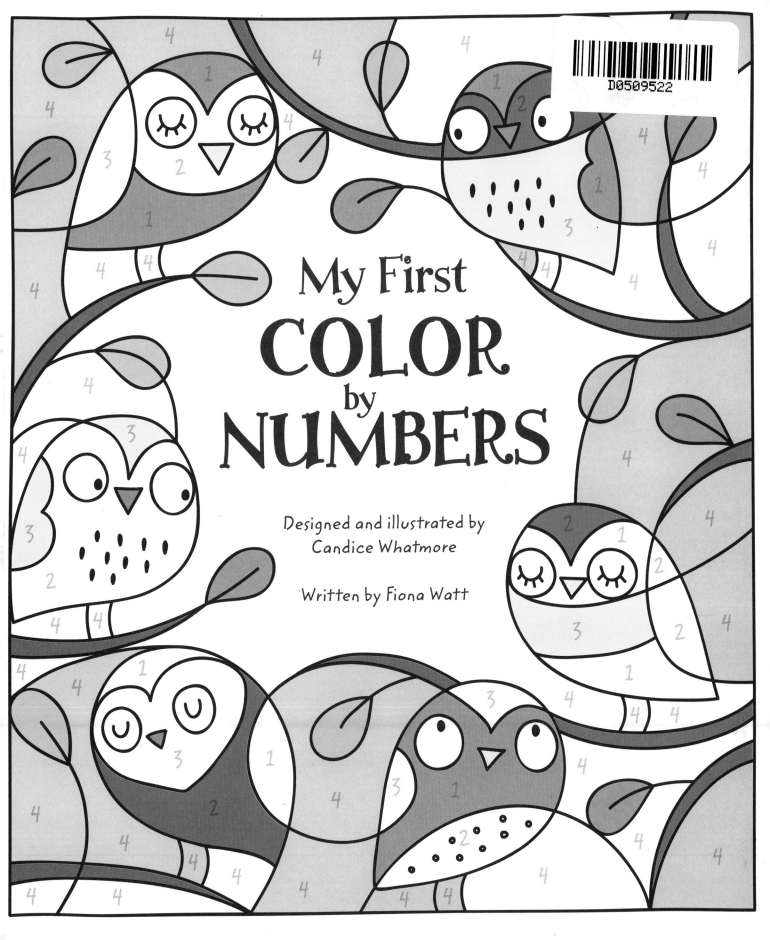

My First
COLOR
by
NUMBERS

Designed and illustrated by
Candice Whatmore

Written by Fiona Watt

How to use this book

On most of the pages you will find a number key that shows you which color to use for each shape.

For example –
1 = ● or red
2 = ● or blue
3 = ○ or yellow

Colored dots

Some of the pages use colored dots as guides instead of numbers. Just color in the shape with the same color as the dot inside it.

If you don't have the correct color of pen or pencil, don't worry. Use another color, but remember which number or colored dot represents the new color.

Color code

1 = ●   2 = ●   3 = ●

Color code

1 = red
2 = yellow
3 = orange

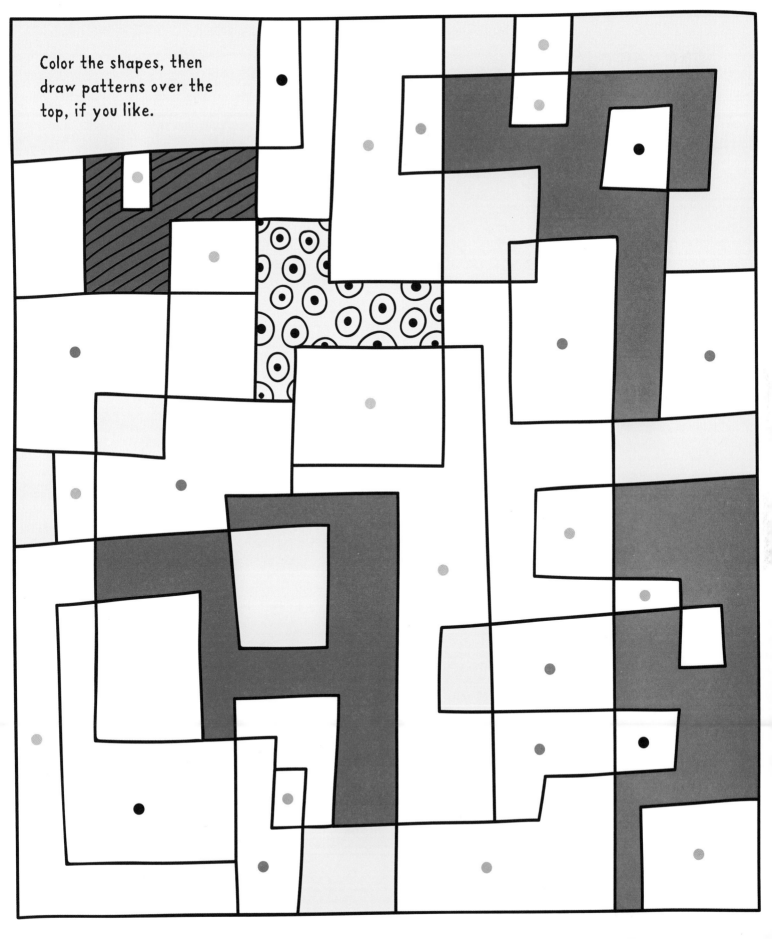

Color the shapes, then draw patterns over the top, if you like.

Color code

1 = ● 2 = ●
3 = ● 4 = ●

Color code
1 = ● 2 = ●
3 = ● 4 = ●

Color code

1 = red   2 = yellow
3 = orange 4 = black
5 = green 6 = gray

Color code

1= red   2= pink

3= orange   4= purple

Color code

1 = purple
2 = black
3 = orange

Color code
1 = ● 2 = ● 3 = ● 4 = ●

Color code
1= ● 2= ● 3= ●

Color code

1 = blue   2 = purple
3 = green   4 = yellow

Color code

1= ● 2= ●
3= ● 4= ●

Color code

1 = red   2 = green
3 = blue   4 = yellow

Color code

1= blue   2= yellow

Color code
1= ● 2= ●

Color code
1= 2=
3= 4=

Color code

1= orange   2= yellow   3= green

Color code   1=● 2=● 3=●

Color code

1= red   2= yellow

3= blue

First published in 2013 by Usborne Publishing Ltd., Usborne House, 83-85 Saffron Hill, London EC1N 8RT, England.

www.usborne.com © 2013 Usborne Publishing Ltd. The name Usborne and the devices 🎈 🌐 are Trade Marks of Usborne Publishing Ltd.